Synecdoche

A Poetry Book
by Margarethe Hattingh

© 2023 Margarethe Hattingh

Publishing label:
ONDALY

ISBN Hardcover: 978-3-903521-03-2
ISBN Softcover: 978-3-903521-02-5

Impressum:
ONDALY GmbH
Mariahilfpark 2
6020 Innsbruck
connect@ondaly.com

Art Direction:
Dagmar Gloning and Amelia Rappl
All rights reserved

This anthology is dedicated to everyone who has known love and loss; hope and disappointment; to everyone who has been afraid.

You are not alone.

Herein —
my heart
Eat of it
what you will.

PART ONE

The Knees of Womanhood

My knees are starting to look a lot like my mother's
Dimpled in some places
Creased in others
Patellas, once sharp,
Have softened with age
Thighs droop now, thickly
Please lower your gaze

A "woman"
Am I
Despite my protestations
Despite my disbelief
In the inevitability of ageing

"Good morning, madam,
How do you do?"

Is it really me
They are talking to?
It must have been the knees
That gave me away

"Good morning, sir,
Just fine. And you?"

Wary of the outward change
I smile sweetly
To mask my shame
Hiding behind my proper ways

Like my mother's skirts of yesterday
Knowing, inside,
I'm just the same

Conscious

I'm a silly, giggly thing
Far too quickly swayed
To rosy complexion
By the noticing of others' harmless
Perception

Who made me so sensitive and caring?
I wish for dullness
Daring
A brutish strength
To meet their gaze

Instead, overwhelmed by conscience,
I turn away
Longing to be seen
But not wanting to be observed
I betray myself
Every day

$\mathcal{I}\ am$ (1)

My body is a library
A collection of memory
Indexed poorly by a child
Still learning to read properly
Silently,
Alone

My mind is a garden
Of half-tended ideas
Growing unruly out of my ears
Planted there by somebody else
In a soil of desire
Watered on fear

And my heart?
A jammed music box
Choked on hope
And stifled truths
Delighting only in its anguish
It was tucked away
A long time ago
To numb the pain of
Feeling

I am (2)

My body is a history book
An unwritten life
Is pressed between the pages
Of my limbs
Like lightning flashes of a summer gone by
The dead flowers of past experience come to haunt me
With their ethereal beauty
And obvious decay
When I am unsuspecting
Caught in a web of the mundane

"Listen," they whisper
With their petal-soft lips
Scratching the lobe of my mind's inner ear
"To *our* story"

And, as quick as they came, they are lost to me
Blown away on the wind of
scattered attention

And I am left
Groping
for their fragrance
Grasping
at the words to bring memory to life
Once more

Roots

Plant soles of feet
Firmly on Earth

Breathe.

Take root here
Stay.
Reaching awareness
To the Earth's core

Hush.

Spirits are with you
The moon above a glowing orb

Dew drops of wonder coat your tongue
Sweetly
As you awaken from the illusion of difference

Listen:
The trees whisper.

PART TWO

On feelings

I have this funny feeling
inside of me
I think it started
in my stomach
Then slowly crawled up
towards my heart
Where, now, instead of butterflies,
it is expansion
yet emptiness:
Longing

Sometimes I feel it in my lungs –
when my eye falls upon your figure,
my breath catches there.
I don't think it's that I'm broken.
I simply feel
overwhelmingly
incomplete

All I've Known

I'm scared you'll find
The hidden hollow places
I buried long ago
Deep inside my soul
I'm scared you'll fill them
With hope for the better
And tell me I am whole

You see,
I need my hidden hollow places
My wounds are mine alone
I keep them out of sight
So they'll never heal right
And I'll always feel at home
In this broken body I have hated
I have loved
All I've known

Wishing

I wish to walk in your sun
To feel the warmth of your breath
tickle my neck
As you kiss the darkness of your absence
from my skin

I wish to catch
the rays of your laugh
Upon the palms of my hands,
curl them around my fingers,
and braid them into my hair
So that, when I walk, their melody resounds
even without you there

I wish to know if you would let me
steal from your light –
If I should let the phantom flames of love
that have started in my heart
burn out
or burn bright

I wish that you were more
than just a dream
tattooed onto the back of my eyes

I wish that, when I closed them,
I wouldn't have to see
Your unreachable smile

Or wish for you
as if you were the sun
and I were the moon

Because the sun would still rise without the moon's
light
but the moon only shines because the sun burns bright

But what else ought I to do?
I wish for you
and wonder if you are wishing, too

Mirror/Mirror

We spent our nights
Exploring the canvases
Of each other's palms –
Mirrors onto themselves
Onto our own hands

Tracing contours with fingertips
Life-lines with index
Love-lines with pinkie
Pressing soft into hollows
With thumbs
And puckered lips
Not daring to search further
Than this innocent bliss

In those night-time wanderings
I learned the map of your hand,
Brother of mine
By flesh
By heart
I walked its valleys
And gentle hills
Until day broke
Painting the story of my love
On your skin
Invisibly

Over
and over
and over
Again

A Poem for You

I have found happiness
Or maybe it found me

Listen:

Happiness is looking up
at the trees in autumn
Seeing the teetering of multihued leaves
on the brink of falling
from all they have known
to the waiting, solid ground below

It is smiling at strangers passing by
Sharing the little bit of sunshine
we all have inside
A silent exchange –
no words required

It is dancing alone
and off-beat
in your room, in your underwear:
Just moving your feet

It is dark chocolate,
or milk chocolate
whichever you like best
Savouring most of its warmth
then sharing the rest

It is star-gazing
cloud-watching
flower-picking
and first kisses
It is an undying belief
in the power of birthday wishes

It is laughing so hard
you begin to cry

It is knowing who loves you,
and not needing to know why

It is here to discover
You are here for it to find
All you have to do is look closely,
but, mostly,
Don't hide

PART THREE

A poem to the boy who owes my heart some heavy-duty patches
(And soon, before it heals all crooked)

For a while you were happiness
A type I had never tasted before
Somehow familiar –
like nutmeg and cinnamon,
fragrant and warm –
But somehow,
with laughter
words
a body and soul
Your taste was new
This happiness was ...
more

You were like sunshine
that breaks the winter clouds
to kiss a smile onto the cold lips of those passing by
Never would those lips question your motives.
No one asks the Sun
Why?

Somehow, we had met already
When I held your hand in mine
and let my fingertips
glide along the surface of your palm
reading the story etched there, in those lines

I forgot whose skin was my own
Lost in a language no one speaks
never learns
Yet everyone knows

The language of silence
Demands no words

Instead,
it was your eyes that promised galaxies
Your smile that reminded me of honey.
You made me believe I was grasping infinity

Now, it seems
that your smile was too sweet
that your eyes promised too much

You were too kind:
You held me close
telling me I was "beautiful"
that what we had was "magical"
To not be scared
That the last thing you wanted was to hurt me
Telling me you cared

In your arms I closed my eyes
I was blissfully, wilfully blind
As you fed me on a diet of lies

You were soda pop:
Too sweet to be healthy
And artificially bright

The fizzing bubbles of our conversation –
your words –
empty of substance
unbearably light

The taste of your memory, now,
in my mouth is bitter
You taste of metallic sadness:
You are unfamiliar.

Silly me, thinking I was over you

If only I could wound you
The way you've wounded me
If only I could cut deep
The same as you've cut me
Then, perhaps your heart would bleed
Would writhe
Would scream
And beg relief
The same as my heart
Has for you
Since you last ate of it

But, cruel trick of Cupid's bow
His arrow's pierced me alone:
He's let me bleed
But let you go
Without so much as a scratch to show
For how hard I loved you

Like the cat who got the cream
You lick your lips
And wash yourself of me
Fat on knowing
My heart got broke
While you walked free

A Poem for the Flower Girl

With your paper-thin skin and my petal soft lips
I cut right through your feeble defences
Until your heart was mine

I took it, then,
Without second thought
Planting kisses in the hollow left behind
Planting seeds of loneliness to blossom into longing
In the darkness
Left behind

I have it, still,
Your heart. It's mine.
I've tried to fix it many times
But it's still broken from when you walked out
And left it behind
Without saying goodbye

I'll give you back yours if you give me back mine?
I can't keep on living with a stranger's heart on the line
I can't love another with a heart that's not mine

Bouquet

Dandelion roots
grew strong this year
Daffodil heart
bloomed late from fear
My margarite petals
were softened by tears
And nectarine blossoms
no fruit did bear

This bouquet
– all of me, now bare –
For you, I picked
My love, my dear

From a Distance

You looked better in the summer
Hair shorter, skin darker
Eyes brighter
Mischief hanging from your upper lip
Puckered, as it were
To kiss my laughing mouth

You're looking down this winter
I see you drooping
From a distance
With hair longer, tucked behind your ears
Like your hopes
Grown out
Mustn't let them in the way

Next Time

Don't confuse broken feelings
or your ruffled feathers
with broken wings
Nor let the pain dragging you down today
keep you from falling in love again
and again

I promise you'll rediscover the edge of love's cliff
And, when you do stand there once more,
Not quite ready to jump,
Thinking "What if...?"
Think not of the ground below
But of the sky:
the possibilities it holds
The blue —
infinitely wide

I promise you'll touch it
That, one day, it will catch you mid-stride

Next time!
Next time, the sky will catch in your wings
and buoy you up high

Next time you fall
I promise,
you'll fly

PART FOUR

Just an Expression

I wish I could draw:
Give form to my thoughts
Relinquish all the chaos of my imagination
onto a page
for another's to make sense of

I wish I could tap that
boom
bang
clang
The fount of liquid fireworks inside my head
Let drip their colours into
paintings or sketches
Order the obstinate mercury into expression

I wish my fingers would obey
I wish that they could guide
and form
and shape:
I wish that they could squeeze all the world
into the tip of a pencil
the hairs of a paintbrush,
Then use it to
Create

But my fingers don't obey
I think we miscommunicate
I ask my hands to listen
but they protest

So: I wish I could sing
Let the Within
be
Without

Let my body be an instrument to my soul
Reverberating with raw humanity
transmitting through the very air
that envelops us each
a song so sweet
it leaves you pure,
empty

But my voice sits in my mouth like rancid honey
it's taste far from that of a melody

So: I wish I could write
stories so beautiful, poems so wonderful,
they move a reader to tears

I wish I could weave
characters' destinies
into one flawless tapestry
make effective use of hyperbole,
metaphor,
and simile
Know how to turn a story on its head
While still fulfilling a hazily defined
artistic duty

But my whole being itches with frustration
at my ineptitude for creation
It's like trying to find the words
to a language I'm only just beginning to learn

I wish to learn

I wish for my pen to be my brush,
for my soul to be my ink,
and my words to be my voice
As I attempt to order the chaos
of my imagination
into transmittable form

I need not impress
but wish only to express

Musings

Every so often my muse comes to visit
Sits by my ear and whispers her secrets
Tells tales of night
Spirits
The moon
Promises poetry
Sweet and true

A seductress from birth
She coaxes forth verse
Then departs from her prey
Before the poem's consummation

She leaves me in ruins
The poem half-made
I am desperate with longing
Forever her slave

On Being and Becoming

I.

A beatific thing
Is imagined creation

In writing I feel
Empty, yet full
At peace
Yet burning
With yearning
To find the right words
Their perfect home

It's a yearning we share,
the words and I
We come to dine together
On the unforgiving page
Exchanging whispers
and eating of each other's conversation
We grow fat
and strong
Laughing out vowels
And twittering the time away

At once reader and writer
are the words and I
Thick as thieves as we bleed the page
of all it has to say

II.

And still they leave me
Despite my devotion
and our splendid commotion
Only with memories
Soon, again, hungry.

Their ghostly forms are imprinted here
as a testament to our communion

III.

Read these words
with faith
And they will fill you

Empty yourself
as you come to worship at the altar of the page
And you will give them life
And the words will give themselves to you

Sacrifice yourself to the promise of possibility
and you will find yourself
a God
once more

At home
At one
with the strangeness
of it all

The Light Between the Lines

I look for God in another's eyes
But in those limpid pools I find
Only a shadowy lie
Away from which I shy

I cast myself out
Seeking a mirror of truth
Alone

But, wherever I walk, my shadow follows
Tying me down to earth
Weighing me to the forsaken ground
Where no God is to be found

So, I turn to poetry
Looking for the light
Between the lines
Learning, through rhyme
The way to heaven
How to fly

Drunk on words
Those angels' tears
I grow wings
Leaving my shadow far behind
To walk on sky
And live, an instant
As divine

Stillborn

They drip like rubies
They ooze like bile
The poems —
They come as they please
Not caring to appease
My desire for their form

Like living beings
They drink their fill of mama's milk
Then run free
Ecstatic children of hurt and longing
Filled with laughter
And thick with blood
They soil the pages of my books
In their carefree dance of life

I wish I could feel as exquisitely as they
In the trenches of my every day
Instead I write as they like
And am grateful to keep buried
The stillbirths
Out of sight

PART FIVE

On Afternoons

I come to rest guiltlessly
Only in the perfect symmetry
Of the afternoon
Two or three pm, depending on
How much of the morning I slept away
Unintentionally

Teeter-tottering in the centre
Of the waking hours
Measured not in daylight
But by the merciless momentum of the
Ticking clock
I am still

And the Earth, it seems
Holds her breath
For just a little while
Pausing in her dizzy spin
And circumnavigation of the sun
As if to say
It's okay
That I do the same

No longer chasing the morning down
With scalding tea
To stoke the fire of my motivation
Nor leaning into evening
In anticipation of the comfort
Of unremembered dreams

Just yet
I rest a little while
Glad, for now,
To be

On Finding God in Leaves and Trees

I could lose myself in the study of leaves, and trees
Not in the knowledge of their scientific names
Nor of the soils from whence they came
But, rather, simply, I could rest my gaze
On leaves, and trees, 'til the end of my days

What is it, you ask, that compels me to claim
Such a devotion to that which I cannot name?
Why, I am certain you see it, too:
It is God I worship, through and through

Not the man who dwells in the sky
Not he who sits, painted, on clouds up high
But, rather, it is He who lives in the leaves, in their
trees
Who lends them undying majesty
It is He who is carried on the bird's wing
Who colours the sun's setting:
It is God in whom I abide
It is through Him alone that my heart survives

He calls me, daily, to find immortality
in the contemplation of Beauty
Asking nothing in return but devotion, unspoken,
To the Spirit which dwells not only in you, not only in
me
But lives in the leaves, and sits in the trees
And returns our world, rightfully
To primordial Mystery

If only we choose to see

The Colour of the Day

Again I see the leaves turn colour
Vibrant yellows, reds, greens and browns
Like burning embers they fall to the ground,
Not yet snuffed
Cloaking the grey street
In their living-dying promise
Of a barren tomorrow
Reborn in springtime

Again I wait for flowers to come,
The birds to sing
The sun to hail a new summer
As the memory of the first frost fades away
For good

Still, I sit
Patiently
Not tensing against winter
Not shutting myself away in mourning
Just yet
Instead savouring the fall –
It's lively colours, its sorrowful grey
Knowing I'll miss it when spring comes
Again

For Ouma Marlene,
who died in the night **(23.04.2021)**

Spring blossoms slowly,
At first
Shyly tucked
Behind Winter's skirts

And then,
Recognising her own beauty,
She blooms fully
With fanfare
In celebration of herself

Petals dripping like confetti
in the streets
And birds hailing her arrival
From newly green trees

The sun does his part in the ceremony
Kissing open buds tenderly
He bestows his blessing in practised ritual
Having Christened her sisters in the years before
Their hopeful passing

Rest in peace,
Flowers of a season

The Circle of Time

Enter into the circle of time
Gladly
With your heart
Wholly
Knowing you are
At the mercy of
The clock's hands

Carry the weight of your death
Quietly
Let it anchor your earthly soul
Ponder it occasionally
And forgive its inevitability

As it forgives your sins
Eventually

Find your place in time
Knowing you will lose yourself
And forget yourself
All the same
As surely as it will lose you and forget you, too

The Age of Man

Do you see
The boy behind the beard
The youth
Beyond the grey?

Can you feel it, here
Sequestered in your chest
A brotherhood of man
The wisdom that remains
Of all our parents' age?

Look upon your hands:
The lines that groove its palms
Familiar, are they not?
These lines –
They are our bond

And, upon your face
I already trace
The life that is to come
At once we are ancient
and reborn – we are young

In your eyes
I see my own
Sharing in this moment
We are together
No less each other
No more alone

'No Time to Rush'

All my life
I spent waiting for time
To catch me in its perfect moment

I am thrifty with my days
Yet look for time in the priciest places
Not realising as it passes by
Before my eyes
Hidden behind inviting smiles
And speckles of wintertime sunshine

Now, I willingly cast my gaze aside
To let time take me by surprise

Margarethe Hattingh is a South African citizen who is lucky enough to have had the opportunity to live abroad most of her life. She currently resides in Vienna, where she would like to stay for at least a little while longer, if the government will let her. Synecdoche is her first published book of poetry. It is something of a coming-of-age story as it is made up of poems written during that tender yet courageous time between the ages of 17 and 23. In addition to Synecdoche, you can find selected poems of hers read out on her YouTube channel "Curation".

Zeitfracht Medien GmbH
Ferdinand-Jühlke-Straße 7
99095 Erfurt, Deutschland
produktsicherheit@kolibri360.de